Exploremos la galaxia/Exploring the Galaxy

Venus/Venus

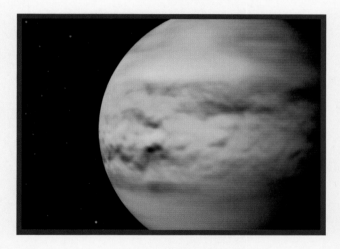

por/by Thomas K. Adamson

Traducción/Translation: Martín Luis Guzmán Ferrer, Ph.D.
Editor Consultor/Consulting Editor: Dra. Gail Saunders-Smith

James Gerard, Consultant
Aerospace Education Specialist, NASA
Kennedy Space Center, Florida

Capstone
press

Mankato, Minnesota

Pebble Plus is published by Capstone Press
151 Good Counsel Drive, P.O. Box 669, Mankato, Minnesota 56002
http://www.capstone-press.com

1 2 3 4 5 6 11 10 09 08 07 06

Library of Congress Cataloging-in-Publication Data
Adamson, Thomas K.
    [Venus. Spanish & English]
    Venus = Venus / by Thomas K. Adamson.
    p. cm.—(Pebble plus: Exploremos la galaxia = Exploring the galaxy)
    English and Spanish.
    Includes index.
    ISBN-13: 978-0-7368-5886-1 (hardcover)
    ISBN-10: 0-7368-5886-5 (hardcover)
    1. Venus (Planet)—Juvenile literature. I. Title. II. Series.
QB621.A3318 2004
523.42—dc22   2005019046

Summary: Simple text and photographs describe the planet Venus.

Editorial Credits
Mari C. Schuh, editor; Kia Adams, designer; Alta Schaffer, photo researcher; Eida del Risco, Spanish copy editor; Jenny Marks, bilingual editor

Photo Credits
Digital Vision, cover, 5 (Venus), 7, 9 (Venus), 15
NASA, 4 (Pluto), 17; JPL, 5 (Jupiter); JPL/Caltech, 5 (Uranus)
PhotoDisc Inc., 4 (Neptune), 5 (Mars, Mercury, Earth, Sun, Saturn), 9 (Earth), 13; Stock Trek, 11; PhotoDisc Imaging, 1, 19
Photo Researchers, Inc./Jerry Schad, 21

Note to Parents and Teachers

The Exploremos la galaxia/Exploring the Galaxy series supports national standards related to earth and space science. This book describes Venus in both English and Spanish. The photographs support early readers and language learners in understanding the text. Repetition of words and phrases helps early readers and language learners learn new words. This book also introduces early readers to subject-specific vocabulary words, which are defined in the Glossary section. Early readers may need assistance to read some words and to use the Table of Contents, Glossary, Internet Sites, and Index sections of the book.

Table of Contents

Tabla de contenidos

Venus

Venus is the second planet
from the Sun. Venus and
the other planets move
around the Sun.

Venus

Venus es el segundo planeta
a partir del Sol. Venus y
los demás planetas se mueven
alrededor del Sol.

The Solar System/El sistema solar

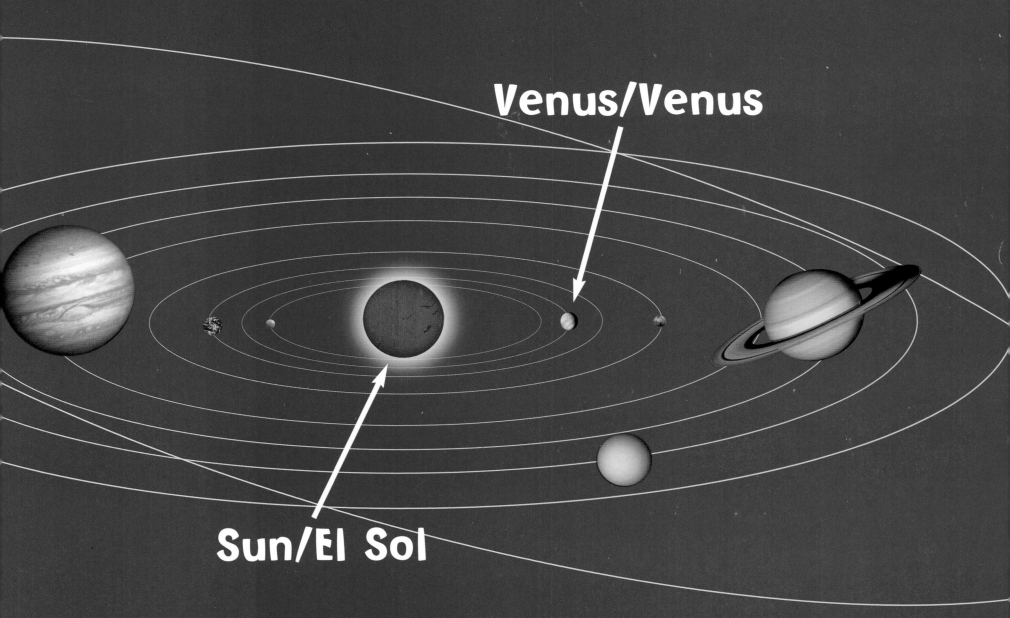

Venus/Venus

Sun/El Sol

Venus is the third brightest
object in the sky. Only
the Sun and Earth's moon
are brighter than Venus.

Venus es el tercer objeto
más brillante en el cielo.
Solamente el Sol y la luna
de la Tierra son más
brillantes que Venus.

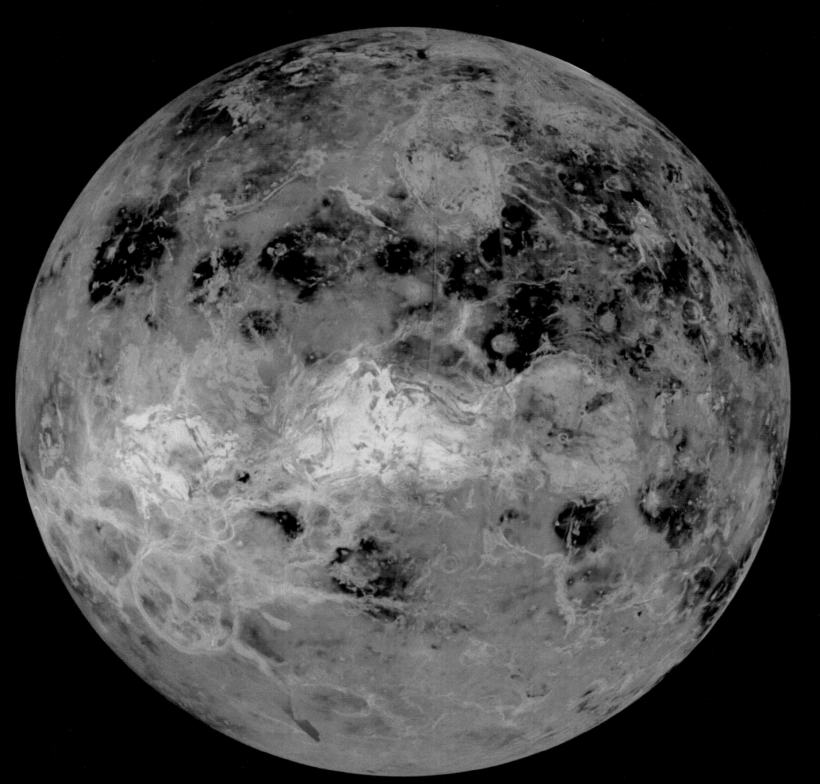

Size of Venus

Venus is almost the
same size as Earth.

El tamaño de Venus

Venus es casi del mismo
tamaño que la Tierra.

Earth/La Tierra

Venus/Venus

Air and Land

Venus is the hottest planet.
The surface of Venus
is hotter than an oven.

Aire y tierra

Venus es el planeta más caliente.
La superficie de Venus es más
caliente que un horno.

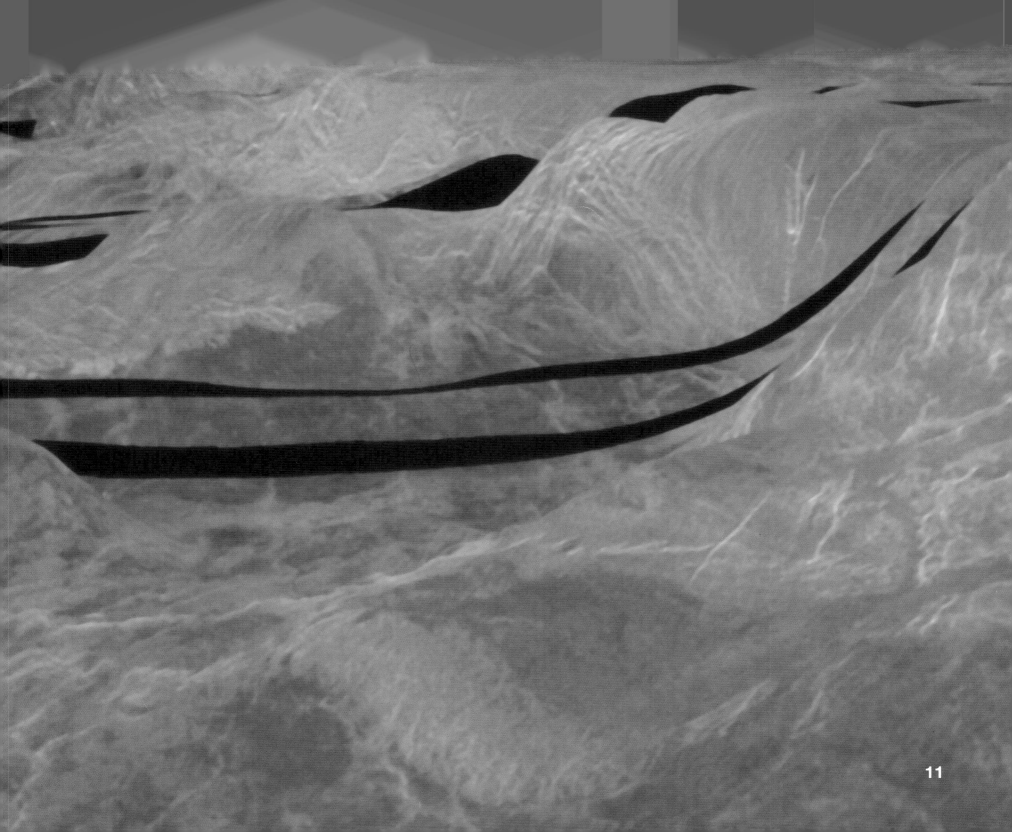

Venus has hundreds
of volcanoes. Thousands of
craters cover Venus.

Venus tiene cientos
de volcanes. Cientos
de cráteres cubren a Venus.

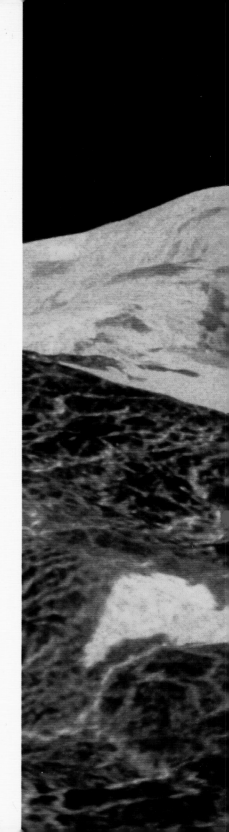

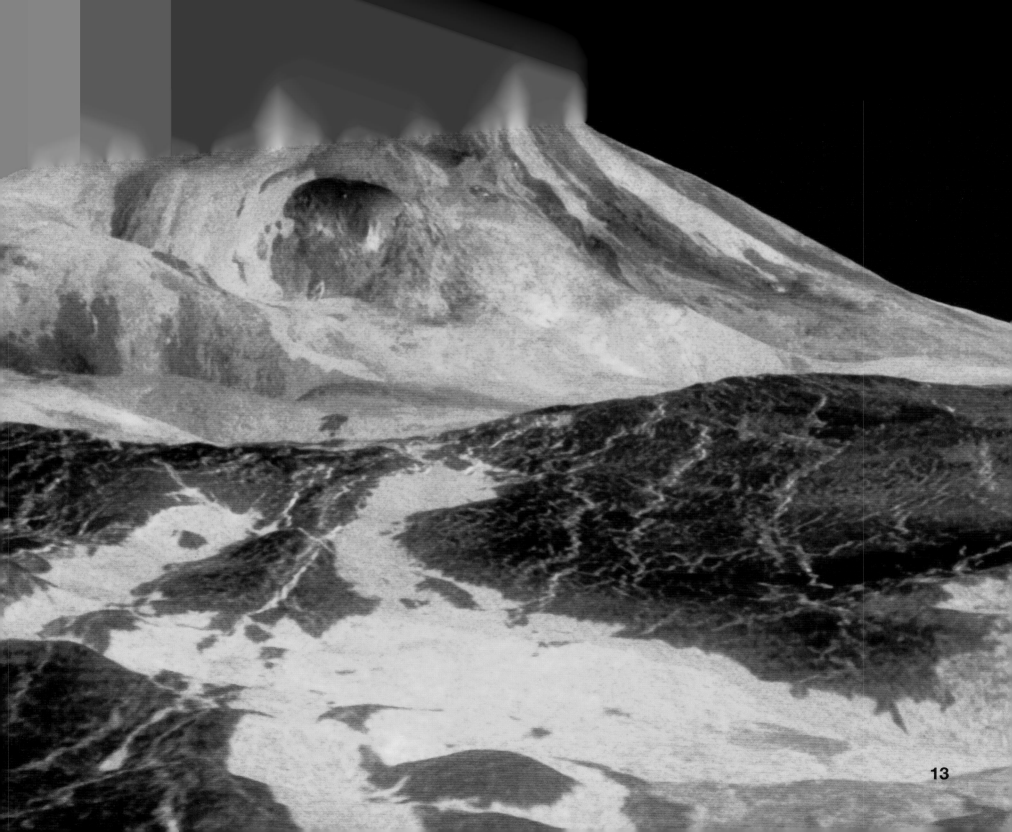

Thick clouds made
of acid cover Venus.

Densas nubes hechas
de ácido cubren a Venus.

The clouds on Venus trap
the Sun's heat. The clouds
make the air heavy.

Las nubes en Venus atrapan
el calor del Sol. Las nubes
hacen que el aire sea pesado.

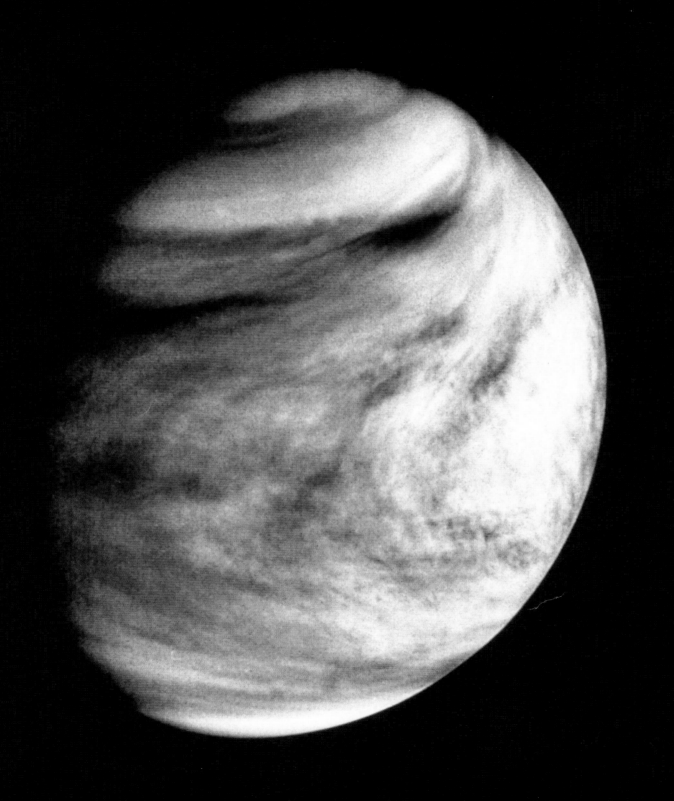

People and Venus

People cannot live on
Venus. The heat would
cook them. The heavy air
would crush them.

La gente y Venus

La gente no puede vivir en
Venus. El calor los cocinaría.
El aire pesado de Venus
los aplastaría.

People can sometimes see
Venus from Earth. Venus
looks like a bright star.

Desde la Tierra, se puede
ver algunas veces a Venus.
Venus parece una estrella
brillante.

Glossary

acid—a substance that can harm people

crater—a large hole in the ground; many craters on planets are caused by falling pieces of rock.

oven—an enclosed space, like a stove, where people bake or roast food

planet—a large object that moves around the Sun; Venus is closer to the Sun than Earth is.

Sun—the star that the planets move around; the Sun provides light and heat for the planets.

volcano—a mountain with vents; melted rock oozes out of the vents; volcanoes on Venus are no longer active.

Glosario

ácido—una sustancia que puede hacerle daño a la gente

cráter—un hoyo grande en la tierra; muchos de los cráteres de los planetas se forman a causa de los pedazos de rocas que caen.

horno—un espacio cerrado, como una estufa, donde la gente hornea o asa la comida

planeta—un objeto grande que se mueve alrededor del Sol; Venus está más cerca del Sol que la Tierra.

Sol—la estrella alrededor de la cual se mueven los planetas; el Sol proporciona luz y calor a los planetas.

volcán—una montaña con respiraderos; rocas derretidas fluyen por los respiraderos; los volcanes de Venus ya no están activos.

Internet Sites

Do you want to find out more about Venus and the solar system? Let FactHound, our fact-finding hound dog, do the research for you.

Here's how:

1) Visit **www.facthound.com**

2) Type in the **Book ID** number: **0736821198**

3) Click on **FETCH IT**.

FactHound will fetch Internet sites picked by our editors just for you!

Sitios de Internet

¿Quieres saber más sobre Venus y el sistema solar? Deja que FactHound, nuestro perro sabueso, haga la investigación por ti.

Así:

1) Ve a **www.facthound.com**

2) Teclea el número ID del libro: **0736821198**

3) Clic en **FETCH IT**.

¡Facthound buscará en los sitios de Internet que han seleccionado nuestros editores sólo para ti!

Index

Índice